BEFORE
and
AFTER

A practical guide for what to do and not to do before and after a loved one dies

---

J.H. "SPIKE" SPEICHER

Before and After

ISBN 978-1-7950552-5-3

Published by

Big Hat Press
Lafayette, California
www.bighatpress.com

TABLE OF CONTENTS

In June, 2017, my wife Linda was diagnosed with lung cancer. She was 74 and a non-smoker except for a short time in college. She died that October. We had been married 54 years. In the weeks and months following her diagnosis, we devoted all our energies to fighting her disease. What we didn't consider was the impact her death would have on our family and her friends. This is the story of what we did do and what we should have done.

—— BEFORE ——

A discussion about what to do when someone is seriously ill normally waits until it is too late. Not having a clear understanding of what to do and how and when to do it can have serious emotional and financial implications.

> **What to do and not do before and after the death of a loved one**

This guide is not just for baby boomers and senior citizens. It is for any age group. Everyone knows of somebody who died too young. The cause could be anything-cancer, an automobile accident, a fall from a ladder or any of a multitude of reasons.

The information contained here can be utilized for you, your parents or other relatives. It can be a guideline for discussions that many parents are reluctant to have with their children.

After Linda's diagnosis, our family focus turned to "we are going to beat this." Even though my son, a doctor, told me that she had stage four lung cancer before we knew it, my thoughts and those of our children were positive. We set a plan of attack with her team of doctors and began treatment. The downside was just too disturbing to think or talk about. This turned out to be a critical mistake.

What to do if Linda died and how to cope with the paperwork was definitely on the "back burner." Little did I know how important it was to get information from her before she went downhill and was unable to communicate.

My wife had her own successful interior design business, which complicated the paperwork challenges. She was a sole proprietor and worked very hard but paperwork was not her strong suit. Thank goodness she had a bookkeeper who was amazing at keeping her on track and profitable. Without the bookkeeper's expertise and assistance, closing Linda's business and preparing the final profit and loss statements for the IRS would have been almost impossible. It was Linda's business and I had little to do with the day to day activities. As I now realize, I should have taken more interest.

Information is power when confronting all of the various public and private organizations and government agencies. Doing something wrong or not doing something that is necessary can affect your financial well-being. Even worse, it may cause governmental penalties, reduce your credit rating or require you to retain highly compensated certified public accountants, lawyers or financial consultants. I met one woman at a grief workshop whose husband died nine years before. She was still trying to close limited partnerships that her husband had accumulated. He had no idea he had made his death so complicated. She was spending a small fortune on financial and legal professionals.

I'm not an expert in any step of this difficult journey, but I've recently been through this emotional time in my life. I hope my advice is of help.

> **"What the hell do I do now?" Your friends do not know what to say.**

There is substantial help on many different fronts when a loved one is ill. The medical community offers help both from a medical and an emotional standpoint. Listen to your doctors, have someone with you to take notes or record meetings. Your mind is swimming and it is difficult to focus with everything going on.

There are many support groups such as the American Cancer Society, Alzheimer's Association and Dementia Association which target specific illnesses. They can supply vast amounts of information.

The internet can supply even more information on the specific illness or condition. In fact, the internet can, at times, supply too much information. Do not get too focused on internet research. It can be overwhelming and time consuming. If you have the chance to meet with others whose loved ones are meeting the same challenge, do it. They can also be a pipeline to new drugs and possible clinical trials.

Some medical organizations are better than others. Again, talk to family, friends and medical personnel you trust to find the best quality hospitals and doctors. Your primary care physician can assist you by recommending specialists.

When using the Internet, look for scientific papers written by specialists in the field. Look under every rock. Somewhere there may be a potential cure. If not a cure, maybe there is a way to prolong life without reducing your loved one's quality of life.

You need to be aware that a vast majority of the medical and professional support vanishes when you hear the doctors tell you, "There is nothing more we can do." No one wants to hear those words. We were devastated when we heard those exact words concerning my wife's terminal illness.

This is the time when palliative care becomes an option if it hasn't already been addressed. This care depends on how your loved one wants to spend the remainder of their life. Groups like Hospice, Vitas and The National Hospice and Palliative Care Organization can be valuable resources.

If you use any of these types of organizations, make sure you check references carefully. Just like any service company, some are better than others.

In our situation, Hospice was the critical link in making sure my wife was well cared for, comfortable and pain free in her last days.

After such incredible focus on trying to get my wife better, a huge void developed after her death. The medical community support was no longer needed, Hospice removed all of the equipment, and life went on except for my loved one.

You wander around the house, seeing reminders of your loved one everywhere and wondering "what the hell do I do now." Your friends stop by and do not know what to say.

They did not know the extent of my grief. The grief was mine and mine alone.

So, now what?

The paperwork avalanche was about to begin. It is a huge challenge. It will be one of the toughest jobs you have ever encountered. My goal in writing this pamphlet is to help you plan **before** your loved one passes away. The important operative word here is "before." You will be better equipped to attack the paperwork if you and your loved one have had candid discussions throughout the years. These are especially important toward the end of life.

The actions you take after death are equally important. The last part of this guide discusses what needs to be done after your loved one dies.

> **Linda and I really wished we had done more communicating and planning earlier in our marriage.**

As it turns out, Linda and I did have some discussions but not enough and definitely not detailed enough. I hope you can learn from our lack of knowledge, effort and communication.

AT ANY TIME OF LIFE, DISASTERS CAN HAPPEN

When I began writing this guide, I felt my audience would be senior citizens who, like me, had lost a loved one. After I lost my wife, I became aware of others of my age group in the same emotional state of grief. I felt my writing would be of help to me and others as I went through the grieving process. My initial effort was a two page write-up with some basic information for someone in my circumstances. Then I joined a grief support group through my church. There were 10 women and two men including me. The women, for the most part, were in serious grief and denial. I gave everyone a copy of my two page write-up. After they read it, most of them said they wished they had it before their spouse passed away. After those comments, I began to gather more information and started expanding my writing.

Later, I met a woman who lost her husband when she was 30 years old and pregnant with their first child. Now, she was single with a young child and no idea what to do. She and her husband were planning their life together, not realizing how soon circumstances would change so quickly and dramatically.

It is hard to imagine but life planning, honest communications and documentation should begin soon after one's honeymoon. That statement sounds extreme and I agree. However, early steps such as creating a will, durable power of attorney, and a durable power of attorney for healthcare can and should be completed at any time. The sooner the better.

My financial advisor had a client who was hit by a truck and sustained serious head injuries. Since he and his wife had no will or durable power of attorney, a judge appointed an executor to manage his affairs. The attorney appointed would not allow any money to flow to the man's wife without going back to the judge every time for permission. It took two years for the wife to get control of their estate. During the two years, the attorney was billing the estate as often as he could. I believe this situation was an exception rather than the norm but it is another potential reason for having a will and/or trust.

PLAN EARLY AND RE-PLAN OFTEN

No one plans early for situations such as what happened in our family. It is always something to put on a to-do list for later. As I have talked to many people who have experienced a loss such as ours, the first comment I hear is **"yes, I know we should have done a better job of planning."** In our journey, both Linda and I wished we had done more communicating and planning earlier.

Lack of preparation is especially apparent in the younger generations. "We are fine; nothing is going to happen to us." But bad things can happen at any time.

I must sound like a messenger of doom. But after living from day to day, month to month after my wife's death, I speak with some authority. If I can help you be better prepared to manage your situation, I've done the job I set out to do.

WILLS/TRUSTS AND DURABLE POWERS OF ATTORNEY

I recently talked with a friend in the Midwest who is with a title company. He gave me a surprising statistic. In the six-county Chicago area, a survey done some years ago found that 46% of the people who had federal taxable estates died without a will and/or trust. That's an amazing number.

Since the survey was done, the threshold for federal taxable estates has risen to an amount that reduces the pressure on many people, wills and trusts are still important for everyone, especially couples with children.

My friend went on to say in situations where there is no will and/or trust, a certified public accountant is needed to finalize the confusing governmental reporting, IRS reporting and other miscellaneous forms required after someone dies.

> **I am amazed but no longer surprised at the high percentage of people who do not have a will or trust.**

Everyone should have a will and/or trust. If someone dies who had neither, the estate must go to Probate. Do you want judges and lawyers (expensive) to make decisions for you and your estate? Absolutely not. Do you want a judge or lawyer making decisions as to who will raise minor children? I have heard many stories about a husband and wife dying in an automobile accident without a will or trust, and the rest of the family arguing as to who will raise the minor children. Whether you are 20, 30, 40, 50 or 60 years old, you need your wishes declared in a will and/ or trust.

Do your homework to find a competent trust attorney. Make basic decisions about who will be executor or guardian of minor children, what assets go to whom, and end of life medical decisions before meeting with the attorney. The financial billing meter begins when you enter the attorney's office. The more homework you do the better.

If you have a joint trust and one of the trustees dies, one of the new burdens on the survivor is to file a tax return every year. You need to apply for and receive a tax ID number for the trust. Your trust attorney can assist you in applying for the tax ID number. All the rules and regulations for an individual tax return apply to the trust.

One other important document you should have your trust attorney prepare is an advance healthcare directive. You have the right to give instructions about your own health care. You also have the right to name someone else to make health care decisions for you. The healthcare directive form lets you do either or both of these things. It also lets you express your wishes regarding the donation of organs and the designation of your primary physician. Make sure your medical professionals and facilities have copies of these documents.

If your spouse passes away, your will/trust will need to be updated.

I was at a party recently and talked with a neighbor. He asked how I was doing now that some time had passed since my wife's death. I told him I was getting better. As a point of discussion, I asked him whether he had a will or trust. He looked at me and said, "No, I have neither."

The surprising fact is that he is a successful owner of a million dollar business with attorneys and CPA's to assist him in his business affairs, but they and he have never taken steps to solidify his personal situation.

I may have been a bit forceful in telling him about how he was doing a disservice to himself, his second wife, both sets of children and his business. If his employees knew about this lack of a will, they would be as nervous as I was. I'll be calling him to see how he progresses on preparing a will. I recently saw his wife, and we discussed his lack of effort. When I told her I would keep calling him until he completed a will, she was all for me keeping the pressure on him.

As I continue to discuss this pamphlet with others, I am amazed but no longer surprised at the high percentage of people who do not have a will or trust. If you are in this category, set a goal today to save your family from trouble, cost and time.

Another step you need to accomplish is the preparing a durable power of attorney and a durable power of attorney for health care. Again, these documents will assist your family in case you are incapacitated. Your trust attorney can assist you in completing these documents. Sample documents can be provided by your medical professionals or medical facilities.

Another thing to remember about wills and trusts is to revise them should the surviving spouse move to a different state. A surviving spouse may want to move to be closer to his or her family. Rules and regulations concerning wills/trusts vary from state to state.

WHERE ARE YOUR DOCUMENTS AND CONTACT INFORMATION?

From discussions with friends, I have learned that people keep their documents in the strangest places or else have no idea where they are. Does this sound familiar?

I had dinner with a couple from Oregon and mentioned some of my experiences before and after my wife died. I mentioned looking for my wife's life insurance policy which I found after some time and searching. The next morning, the doorbell rang and there were my friends. They asked for a copy of my write-up and then told me that before going to bed after dinner the night before, they both looked at each other and asked the same question, "Do you know where our life insurance policies are?" When they arrived home, they found them. The life insurance policies are important documents, but equally important is to have records of the policy numbers and the 800 telephone number for the insurance company.

Insurance agents advise their clients not to place insurance policies in a safety deposit box. A policy is your receipt that your loved one was insured. After the death of your loved one, you may not be able to get the policy quickly especially if you do not know where the safety deposit box key is. Equally important, do you know the name of the financial institution and where the branch is located?

Where are your important documents? Are they easy to get to? Are all documents in one location? Are they well organized? Are they updated on a periodic basis? Do the children or other relatives know where they are? (More about this question later)

CHALLENGES OF A DIGITAL WORLD

At all times, make sure the lines of communication are wide open between your loved one and your entire family. This is one of the most critical steps that should be taken, especially before a loved one is too ill to communicate. I know it is tough, really tough to talk about end of life decisions, but information is very important in today's digital world.

> **As difficult as it may be, you need to communicate with your loved one and get all of his/her digital information.**

Today, the center of everyone's financial world is the internet. Within this new world, it is critically important to gather all of the following information. As difficult as it may be, you need to communicate with your loved one and get all of his/her digital information. This discussion will save time and effort in the long run. This information includes:

User names and passwords are needed for all financial accounts. The same holds true for apps. Companies are important if you use the internet to pay bills on line. Keep the list up to date when you change user names and/or passwords. If you add accounts or apps, make sure your list is updated.

Internet accounts for email also need to be tracked. If bills or invoices are sent by email to your loved one, you need to know it. About three months after my wife died, I received a letter from one of my utility companies. It stated that I had 48 hours to pay my bill or my electricity and gas would be shut off. I had not received a bill. After doing research and spending quite a bit of time, I found that my wife had the bill sent by email. Since I had her email user name and password, I was able to find the bill. After I paid, I went onto the company's website and made the necessary changes so I now receive the bill on-line. I then checked our other on-line accounts to make sure I had no other surprises. Unpaid bills can affect your credit rating or cause expensive late charges.

By having all of your loved one's digital information, you eliminate the possibility making a decision that could be wrong or cause you to lose benefits or money.

If the automatic bill payment feature has been used by your loved one, you need to change and update the accounts to a valid credit card. If the automatic bill payment feature was being debited to a bank checking account, make sure the bank has not cancelled the account. This could happen if the checking account was only in the name of your loved one.

User names and passwords for sites such as Facebook must also be included. I know of situations where a family wanted to inform friends who use Facebook about their loved one's passing but were unable to do so. The Facebook account is out there, and I guess will be there forever.

I talked to one couple who shared their financial chores by being responsible for monitoring and paying bills on alternate years. That way, both of them knew the importance of being up to date, digitally speaking.

There are a number of apps and programs that will store your many user names and passwords in an ultra-secure file. If you use such an app, make sure you and members of your family have the secure password.

ORGANIZING AND COMMUNICATING INFORMATION ABOUT YOUR FINANCIAL LIFE

Your financial life is even more important if you and your loved one have retired. Living on a fixed income can be a challenge. Do you have enough money to keep you in your home, enjoy travel, and hopefully have some inheritance for your children or other life objectives? You need a financial plan or written strategy moving forward.

Most families have no plan. A recent *Wall Street Journal* article was more specific. "According to the Transamerica Center for Retirement Studies, only 11% of workers over age 65 have a written strategy or financial plan for retirement."

Catherine Collinson, President of the Transamerica Center for Retirement Studies, stated that "A written financial plan for retirement is like a reality check to ensure you're financially ready to retire."

If you do not have a financial plan when a loved one passes away, one of the first objectives should be the development of a plan looking forward to being alone. If you do have a plan, meet with your financial advisor to review and amend it after the death of your loved one.

You need to especially look at your sources of income. If your loved one received Social Security, that income goes away. If your loved one was still working, that income goes away. Will you have enough other income to live comfortably?

You and your children need to know whether you will be OK. If you have a financial plan, it should be updated to reflect your new situation. If you do not have a plan, make one. The rest of this section gives you an outline of what one of my friends did for her family.

My close friend, Peggy Cabaniss, is a retired Certified Financial Advisor. She and my wife and another girlfriend talked and walked every weekend for years. When my wife died, Peggy realized that she and her husband needed to open the lines of communication with their three adult children and have a family meeting to discuss their financial plan. So she and her husband planned a full day meeting with an agenda and financial information.

> **If you do not have a financial plan when a loved one passes away, one of the first objectives should be the development of one.**

The children flew in on a Friday from their homes across the country. Peggy and her husband paid for their flights. They had a nice dinner Friday night and started their meeting on Saturday morning.

A pre-meeting questionnaire was emailed to each child asking the following questions:

1. What do I hope to learn from this first family meeting?
2. What issues do I have that I need and want to discuss?

The following agenda was presented. It must be noted that spouses of the children were not invited.

7:30am	*Family breakfast*
8:30am	*Ground rules, schedule, note taker/scribe for "Action Items"*
9:00am	*Assets, net worth, allocations, holdings-review what we own, where it is held, how to get access to it, valuation*
10:00am	*The Estate Plans-Review the trust, will, durable power of attorney for healthcare, and other directives*
11:00am	*The children's estate plans-What needs to be considered in light of their own assets as well as any possible inheritance*
11:30am	*Break time*
12:30pm	*Lunch*
1:30pm	*Health Care and Aging Issues*
	Doctors, medicines, medical records
	Advance Directives
	Paying for long term care-Insurance, Assets, Social Security
	Who will be involved in health care issues?
	Housing Issues-Preferences, Possibilities, and Possible Problems

2:30pm	Final Arrangements-Burial, Cremation/Place/ Service/Wishes
3:30pm	Digital Estate-What to do about Digital Records, Passwords, On-line Accounts, etc.
4:30pm	Where are all the papers?

Identification documents

Insurance Policies

Financial Information

Contacts

Odds and Ends

5:30pm	Wine and Cheese

Family Values- A discussion of what each member of the family feels is important in terms of values, how they want to live now, what the family wants to pass on to the children, what has been passed on to the family already from the parents and grandparents.

There was also a discussion of possible conflicts and ways to resolve them.

7:00pm	Family Dinner

Next Morning

7:00am	Family Breakfast
8:00am	Open discussion and comments about the weekend, suggestions for the next time, review list of "Action Items" and responsibilities for completion of those items.

Peggy and her husband felt the weekend brought the immediate family closer together. The children were grateful for all of the information and felt a big relief knowing it. All three of the children had been worried as to whether Mom and Dad had enough money to last through their remaining years. The meeting gave them a sense of relief.

Peggy created a binder for the children.

TAB I

　　1. Agenda for the day

　　2. Email response from the children's original questions

TAB II

　　3. Statement of Net Worth including allocation of assets

　　4. Investment Account Statements

　　5. Tax Returns - (Sample of a recent good year, sample of a bad year). The returns were the basis for a discussion to show that not all years are good or bad

　　6. Cash Flow Forecast-Show simple method of calculating income and expenses for the year

TAB III

　　7. Copy of Trust Document

　　8. Flowchart of Overall Distribution Plan

TAB IV

9. Miscellaneous Trust Documents-Certifications of Trust, Bill of Transfer, Statement of Community Property, etc.

TAB V

10. Copies of Durable Power of Attorney

11. Copies of Durable Power of Attorney for Health Care

TAB VI

12. List of Important Documents and Location in the House/Files

13. List of Valuables throughout the House

14. Insurance Summary-All policies, limits, policy Number, Premium

15. Digital Records-List of all Accounts, Passwords (Showed them the Report but not included in their Binder to Take Home)

TAB VII

16. General articles about Estate Planning, Family Meetings and Checklists of "What to do When Someone Dies"

A family meeting is an effective way to bring your adult children up to date on your financial life. This is also an effective method to enable your own parents to explain their financial situation to you, if they are reluctant to do so. I recommend a family meeting on a periodic basis, especially if there is a change in the family dynamics.

You may not want to be this detailed in what you discuss with your children, but what Peggy developed is a great guide to help you begin.

If you feel there may be disagreements or conflict between your children, there are psychologists that specialize in conflict management. These professionals can be ideal facilitators especially if you think there will be heated discussions in the future. It is best to resolve conflicts earlier than later.

Another important communication topic was suggested to me by a friend's adult son. He felt he needed to know the medical history of the family tree, especially the cause of each person's death and the age at which that relative died. He said that doctors ask these types of questions as part of gathering patients medical history. The son felt he knew very little about his past family's medical history.

I had a friend tell me that when discussing medical histories, it is a great time to share stories about parents, grandparents, aunts and uncles. These kinds of discussions give the next generation a sense of their family's history.

POINTS ARE NOT YOUR PROPERTY

This title is actually part of one credit card company's agreement.

There is a love-hate relationship with credit card companies. You love them for their convenience but hate them for the rules and regulations. Does anyone actually read their agreements?

This section may be the most important section in this guide. It focuses on what should be done with credit card accounts that have points or miles associated with them **before** your loved one passes away.

The most critical thing before and after your loved one passes away is to do nothing that involves credit cards and money associated with them. Do not, and I repeat, do not cancel credit cards until you research the account and see where you are. Be very careful if you call any credit card company or financial institution. If you tell them your loved one has passed away, the first thing they will do after saying "I'm so sorry for your loss" is to ask you for the credit card number. If you give the number to them, they immediately cancel the account. If they ask for the number, hang up. Do not talk with the credit card company until your research is completed.

> **What should be done with credit card accounts that have points or miles associated with them BEFORE your loved one passes away may be the most important section in this guide.**

A credit card company's secret that they do not discuss is hidden in their card member agreement. This "secret" has to do with their loyalty award points or miles programs. They state in the agreement that "Points are not your property." I disagree. Points have been awarded to you or your loved one, the card holder. You earned those points and/or miles

So, let's take a close look at what this means. If you make a mistake and cancel a credit card that has points or miles connected to it, those points or miles may be immediately canceled. That is a real win for the credit card company. They have been carrying those award points or miles as a liability owed to the credit card holder. If they cancel them, there is no obligation to award those points or miles to anyone.

Each credit card company may have different rules concerning the loyalty points or miles. Each airline also has different rules. Some airline programs allow you to transfer points or miles to another person. Others will do a transfer but will charge a transfer fee. Still others absolutely refuse to transfer points or miles.

One airline loyalty program agreement states, "Points aren't your property and have no cash value. Additionally, points can't be transferred by operation of law, such as by inheritance, in bankruptcy or in connection with a divorce." Though it is not stated directly, this also includes the death of the loyalty program member. I recently found this statement in another credit card's solicitation "Your rewards are yours for the life of the account-they will not expire. But if your account is closed, you will lose any rewards you have not redeemed." **This includes any account**

closed because of the death of the primary card holder unless it is a joint credit card account.

If an airline allows for the transfer of points or miles to another person, they may ask for a copy of a death certificate.

I have heard situations where a person designates someone to receive the points or miles in their will. The important takeaway from this section is to research each credit card company and airline to make sure you do not lose any value after your loved one passes away. When in doubt, use the awards before death occurs.

This is a major reason to make sure you have all user names and password for your loved one's credit card accounts. You need to know them early enough to check for points or miles before your loved one dies. Then take advantage of the points or miles for merchandise or travel using their reward partners. Use them or lose them. I know of one family whose loved one specifically asked her family to use the points and miles she had accrued for a European trip to remember her. Arrangements were made and discussed with her before she died. She was very happy to know that her points were going to be used by the family and not cancelled by the credit card company.

Another confusing situation with credit card companies is the definition of the primary holder. If it is a joint card, the credit card is still valid and the points or miles continue to be accrued for the other remaining account holder if one of you should die.

However, if you are an add-on card holder (which credit card companies push in their marketing programs) when the primary card holder dies and you notify the company, you immediately lose the use of the card. The primary account is quickly cancelled. More important, all points or miles may be cancelled.

I have talked with a number of attorneys and financial planners who had no idea that this cancellation of points or miles was written into the credit card company agreements.

I am embarrassed to say I made a mistake and lost quite a few of my wife's points. My wife, as I have said, had her own business and had her financial accounts with a major bank in California. After she passed away, I wanted to cancel her company savings and checking accounts. I was unsuccessful since I was not a signatory for her accounts. Our daughter was, and only she could cancel the accounts. While I was talking to a bank representative, I noticed another representative working on her computer. I asked what she was doing. She said she was cancelling my wife's company credit card. I did not know she had a credit card for her business with this particular bank. The bank's employee commented that she was required to immediately cancel the credit card. I told her to stop. She did not. Because I did not know about that particular credit card account, our family lost a substantial number of points. It was my lack of communication with my wife that cost us this loss.

Another credit card company secret is that if the primary credit card holder passes away, any amount owed on the credit card does not necessarily need to be paid. Check with your legal advisor to see if that holds true for you or your loved one's credit card account. The company will try to have the relatives clear the account but you may not be under any legal obligation to pay it off.

Be very careful in dealing with credit card companies. They are not focused on you, the customer. They are focused strictly on their bottom line.

COMMUNICATING WITH
YOUR PARENTS

As I began writing this pamphlet, I talked to many friends and acquaintances for advice and ideas. One particular generational situation kept coming up. As our generation has grown older, so has our parents' generation. They are living longer, full lives. We have become as they say, the *sandwich generation*. We live in this world of taking care of our parents and

> **Taking care of our parents can be even more difficult than taking care of ourselves.**

also providing for our children should they need help.

Taking care of our parents can be even more difficult than taking care of ourselves. Everything I write about in this guide becomes more of a challenge with our parents. They are reluctant to talk about any problems, especially those involving their financial health.

Many of you are identified in your parents' wills and trusts as the executor of their estate. You may also have the durable power of attorney for your parents. You may also be involved with their living will/durable power of attorney for health care.

Your parents may not be technologically savvy, but they do have financial concerns and holdings that must be discussed and identified should one or both of them begin having medical problems. These include:

Stocks and Bonds

Real Estate

Insurance (Life, Health and Property)

Checking and Savings Accounts

Money Market Accounts

CD's

Credit Cards
(See the discussion of reward points and miles)

You also need names, addresses, telephone numbers and email addresses for all of your parents' financial advisors and professionals.

Every question or statement that I make in this pamphlet needs to be discussed with your aging parents. If you think asking these questions of a sick loved one is difficult, wait until you ask your parents.

You may find surprises in your parents' estate. They may not want to talk about any of this with you. If you get the information before anything serious happens to them, it will make settling their estate easier and less expensive.

AFTER

Medical problems can start at any time, but I am focused on later in life. You may feel like nothing has gone your way if you or your loved one has had a serious diagnosis. You and the family have not gotten a positive break. You've been hearing nothing but bad news.

WHAT TO DO AND NOT DO IMMEDIATELY AFTER THE DEATH OF YOUR LOVED ONE

First and foremost, make no major decisions for at least a year, especially financial ones. You are in no shape emotionally to make critical decisions that will affect the rest of your life. Society applies pressure to get things done and move forward. Resist the outside pressures and move at a pace comfortable to you and your family.

> **First and foremost, make no major decisions for at least a year, especially financial ones.**

The paperwork will be there next week, next month or next year. There are only a few critical decisions that must be made such as government mandates, Internal Revenue Service deadlines and financial deadlines such as Social Security changes.

Soon after my wife died, a cousin with whom I was very close also died. I had a panic call from his wife telling me the bank had cancelled every financial account they had. All of the accounts were in his name (huge mistake) and she had no access to cash, checking account, savings account or credit card. Her daughter was finally able to get the bank to release funds so her mother could survive. It was not an easy task.

Everyone should have at least one credit card in his or her name and use it to build a credit history. Since my cousin's wife was an add-on to every one of his financial accounts and credit cards, she had no credit history. When she applied for a new credit card, she did not exist financially. She was only able to get a credit card with a very low credit limit.

THE FIRST MONTH

You will be overwhelmed, first with making arrangements for the funeral or memorial service. That includes where to have the service, how it will be structured, who will speak at the service and a multitude of other decisions (see next section). Relatives and friends will be flying in and need housing, transportation and meals. Do you use a church or other venue for the funeral or memorial service? What do you serve after the service? Wow, so much to do and little time to do it. Grief has begun but is not a top priority until later.

THOUGHTS FOR A
MEMORIAL SERVICE

After your loved one has passed away, one of the first decisions is whether to have a memorial service or funeral. The family should meet and make the decision and, if yes, then decide on a venue. It could be a church or another building that caters to private events.

The following is a list of some considerations as you plan a memorial service.

Find a venue and make a reservation

Memorial Service Considerations
> Invite those who will participate in the service
> Designate individuals as readers
> Designate speakers for sharing
> Select readings and music
> Contact florist if flowers are to be used
> Contact caterer if food will be served
> Choose a vocalist if music will be involved
> Prepare a memorial bulletin with a photograph

If friends or relatives are going to speak, I suggest that their remarks are written and be very careful to limit their speaking time. A good guideline is that two pages, double-spaced, equals about five minutes of talking time.

I also suggest not having what is known as "open mic time." You have no control over who speaks and for how long. I have attended memorial services that were too long because many friends wanted to talk and they talked for too long.

If a reception is planned, it is helpful to look for a venue near where the memorial service is held.

It is difficult planning a memorial soon after the death of a loved one. Again, ask for help from friends and relatives. If the service is going to be at a church, ask for help from the pastors and lay members of the congregation.

SUPPORT SYSTEM OF FRIENDS, RELATIVES AND HELPFUL ORGANIZATIONS

You will second guess every decision you make. It's a normal reaction. My family and I went down this path many times in the four months between Linda's diagnosis and her death. I was fortunate to have three amazing children who were my rock solid support system. Always ask for help.

> **Do not let yourself be pressured or rushed into your new life. Take your time. Only you know when it is time to move on.**

Life changes dramatically. You are now living in a new normal. It is critically important for you to begin asking for and accepting help from many different sources. These sources include family, close friends, not so close friends, relatives, faith groups and the support organizations that provide services. Always seek assistance from anyone and everyone. Do not go on this journey alone. Ask for help! Someone will be there for you.

Within your local community, you will be surprised how many non-profit and faith based organizations there are that can help you. It just takes a bit of research to find one or two that meet your criteria and then ask for help. Also ask your medical professionals for recommendations.

WHO ARE YOUR REAL FRIENDS?

After the death of a loved one, the outpouring of support and help is amazing. Food shows up at your door, friends run errands for you, and other friends stop by to console you. You and your family are well taken care of. But soon, the focus slips. Friends are busy. They have their own lives to live.

But throughout it all, there are special friends who stay with you. They call, they listen, and they help. For me, the grieving process has continued and in many cases, those special friends have been through the process themselves.

In my case, I have two special friends from my Rotary Club who have both lost their wives. One lost his wife 10 years ago and the other three years ago. They can truly say, "I understand your loss." They know, they understand and can talk frankly with me. They say it will get better and I'm moving in that direction.

> **Through it all, there are special friends who stay with you. They call, they listen and they help.**

If friends invite you to join them for dinner, lunch, coffee or whatever, accept their invitations. If you do not, they will not continue to ask. It is important to be around people. It will be difficult but necessary. It is an important step in the grieving process.

RELATIONSHIP WITH THE MEDICAL COMMUNITY AFTER THE DEATH OF A LOVED ONE

To my wife's primary care physician and specialists, huge thanks are due. In my case, we were referred to many wonderful medical personnel who were part of our action team to assess, recommend, and perform procedures that we hoped would slow or eliminate the progression of her cancer. Make sure you thank your doctors for their great support and care. And don't forget the amazing support given by other medical personnel such as nurses and technicians. Just as important are the administrative personnel who handle the paperwork and get approvals for the procedures during the attempt to beat your loved one's illness. They see life and death every day. They have their own highs and lows. For them, it is more than a job; it is a calling, a mission to save a life.

GRIEF SUPPORT AFTER DEATH

The grief after the loss of a spouse or loved one is much more pronounced than you can imagine. You will be devastated. Sleep is difficult. Getting through the day is even more difficult. Friends and family do not know what to say or how to say it. Only someone who has experienced such a major loss can understand your feelings.

There are many avenues for support. Be proactive and find them. Lean on friends, family, your church and grief support groups. As I mentioned earlier, I joined a grief support group my church sponsored. There were 10 widows and two widowers. We met for two hours for 10 weeks on Tuesday afternoons.

> **Seek professional help, especially if there are decisions needed that would or could affect your new financial situation.**

Spouses had died at various times over the past two years. The first meeting was terrible. The facilitator asked all of us to talk about our loved one and what happened. There were a lot of tears, and I learned more about the circumstances of someone's death than I really needed to know. I thought I would not attend another meeting. But I did attend a second meeting. I did attend all of the meetings. As the meetings progressed, we got to know everyone and then help each other in the grieving process. By the time the 10 weeks were completed, we had become friends. We got together for lunch a few weeks later to see how everyone was doing.

As I talked with other men who had lost their wives, I found many unwilling to join any such group. We guys want to tough it out. That thought process is not healthy but somewhat understandable. Two of my close friends had lost their wives. Because of their experiences, they were of immense help to me during my early months of grieving.

Others may pressure you to "move on" and "get over the grief." They say to start living again. Do not let yourself be pressured or rushed into your new life. Take your time. Only you know when it is time to move on.

Do not attempt to work out your grief alone. It is much too difficult.

REMOVING YOUR LOVED ONE'S POSSESSIONS FROM YOUR HOME

One of the emotional situations that one encounters is the removing of your loved one's clothing and personal items from your home. This is one area where I needed support and help from my children. When it came to clothing, I did not know the difference between an item from GAP and a high end designer. My daughters took over. I was there to help but found out quickly that I was of no help. It was too emotional for me.

My wife had talked with our daughters about her wardrobe and what to do with her gently used clothing. She wanted the local Hospice Thrift Shop to get her clothing. So I delivered many boxes and bags of clothing there.

One major item that I did handle myself was the sale of her car. It was obvious I did not need two cars. I kept mine and sold hers. The money from the car went into my investments.

PROFESSIONAL HELP

Seek professional help, especially if there are decisions needed that would or could affect your new financial situation. I've met too many widows who have no knowledge of their financial situation or how to insure they are financially stable. If your family has worked with a certified financial advisor let that person assist you in making solid decisions to protect the value of the estate.

Professional help is expensive but may be necessary if complex legal or financial issues come up. Professional help may include:

Certified Financial Advisor

Trust/Estate Attorney

Stock Broker

Professional Appraisers (real estate, personal property such as art, jewelry, automobiles, and recreational vehicles)

If your loved one managed all investments, it may now be important to interview and select a Certified Financial Advisor to assist you in managing your new financial life. Ask for recommendations from trusted friends or associates. Interview the recommended advisors and select one sooner than later. You have too much on your mind to be involved in IRA transfers, buy and sell decisions, and the many other financial considerations that need attention.

After attending my church-sponsored grief support group, I realized there is another whole group of professionals needed to support those who have lost their loved one. In this case, the support is needed specifically for women who have lost their husbands. A vast majority of these women still want to stay in their homes and need handyman help for fix-it jobs around the house. They are afraid to have a man they do not know enter their homes to do minor repairs. They are even more afraid to have two repairmen in their homes.

A widow in the support group asked me the following question after one of the meetings. She said "Spike, how do I know if a fire extinguisher is still good?" It was a valid question and I answered it. That opened a floodgate of questions from smoke and carbon dioxide detectors to small plumbing leaks.

I am a member of Rotary International, and our group has a program we call Home Team that works with a senior support organization to handle requests from seniors who need minor repairs. Our Rotarians meet on a Saturday about every four to six weeks, and teams go out to the homes that need basic repairs. We are completely vetted and insured and spend whatever time is needed to complete the repairs. It is a great service for widows and widowers. See if you can find a local organization that does similar work.

LIFE INSURANCE

If your loved one had whole life insurance, one of your first efforts should be to contact your life insurance representative and file a claim form for the proceeds of the policy. An insurance company is one of the few organizations that need an original death certificate. Send it as soon as requested.

It is important to remember that insurance companies have settlement options other than a lump sum payout for the proceeds from insurance policies. As an example, you could ask for a ten-year payout. Another idea is to ask for a checkbook and only use the proceeds when you need to. The remaining proceeds will continue to accrue interest with the company. You should also check the current interest rates earned from both the insurance company and your financial institution. The insurance company rate may be higher. Discuss your options with your insurance agent before taking a lump sum payout. Once you take the settlement, other options are not available.

DEATH CERTIFICATES

Sometimes, it is the little things that really surprise you as you move forward after the loss of your loved one. One of those little surprises is the need for certified death certificates. They are necessary for many of the notifications that you need to make, but be careful how many you order. The funeral home or cremation company will ask you how many you need. Before you answer, you should know they are expensive. In California, as I write this, my county charges $25.00 each.

I recommend ordering no more than 10. I ordered five and still have two left. If you need more, you can order them. There are entities, especially life insurance and mortgage companies and governmental agencies, that need an original certificate. I found that most other organizations need only to see the original and then will make a copy and send the original back to you. Ask for the original back. Though I did not do it, my thought was to include a self-addressed stamped envelope with the original to encourage the receiving company to return it.

FOUND MONEY

As I talked to friends about this pamphlet, a number of them said that they would have the same problems with their fathers and mothers as they would if their spouse died. Many said that their parents would be a bigger problem since they were very reluctant to talk about their life situations. Hopefully many of the ideas and suggestions in this guide will help you when dealing with your parents.

> **We have all heard stories of finding cash in strange places after one passes away.**

If your parents grew in the Depression or soon thereafter, they were involved in one of the nation's worst financial times. We have all heard stories of finding cash in strange places after someone passes away. Elderly people have a tendency to hide cash is a result of growing up during the Depression. They watched their parents struggle, and it made an indelible impression on them. They always felt they needed a stash of money hidden away for a "rainy day."

After the death of his mother, one friend and his sister were cleaning out her closets. What her children planned as a day or two turned out to take over a week. As they began sorting the clothing, one the children checked the pocket of blazer. In the pocket was cash, a lot more than a dollar or two. Every piece of clothing had to be checked, every pocket gone through. They also had to check shoe boxes, shoes and purses for hidden cash. Their mother had Alzheimer's and had no idea where she had hidden money. As it turned out, they found over $5,500.

My friend's father died soon after. He was smart enough to tell his daughter that he also had hidden money. In his case, he had placed $14,000 in an old tackle box and carefully placed it in the rafters of his garage. He also had envelopes hidden in his dresser and other places with even more cash. If he had not told his daughter, that money could have been lost. When asked why he hid the money, his reason was to have cash in case of a serious earthquake. This again shows the critical need to have good communications with your parents.

Another friend put it this way "Know where the treasures are hidden." Treasures can be jewelry, coin collections, stamp collections or any other valuables. Safety deposit boxes are the normal way of protecting and storing such "treasure" but many senior citizens do not use them. They often do not trust banks. If they do use safety deposit boxes, know where the keys are.

Treasures can be many things:

1. Valuable papers and documents

2. Checkbooks, current bank statements

3. The family heirlooms that your loved ones held dear and are sentimentally important

4. Art, china, and sterling silver

THE GOVERNMENT IS WATCHING YOU AND WHAT YOU DO AFTER THE DEATH OF YOUR LOVED ONE

That means all governments, federal, state and local. Governmental forms are many and sometimes confusing. The government is not sympathetic to missed deadlines or excuses.

It all starts when the cremation organization or funeral home notifies the Social Security Administration that your loved one has died. They are required by law to make that notification.

When it is time for preparing yearly tax reports, the problems and nuances of the tax laws become very important. If a trust is involved, it becomes even more confusing. Your trust attorney becomes one of your most important professional experts. It feels like your attorney should be on your speed dial.

One of the first items of business is an application for a tax ID for the trust. The decedent half of the trust has assets that need to be tracked, and if there is any income, it must be reported. Even after death, the government is still looking for tax revenue

Another financial situation where you need professional guidance is dealing with your loved one's IRA, Roth IRA or any other government retirement account. The rules about these accounts are confusing and a mistake can be very costly.

Again, this is the time for professional help. Your tax preparer or tax attorney has dealt with these requirements many times. They know what to do and how to do it. Rely on them to keep you out of trouble with the authorities.

A SPOUSAL BUSINESS
ADDS COMPLEXITY

My wife's successful interior design business spanned more than 33 years. She had a wonderful design and color sense and had many clients, some as far away as New Mexico, Michigan, and the East Coast. Hers was a sole proprietorship. I had little to do with her business. After she died in October, 2017, I decided to close the business by the end of the year. We had to keep the business open until the end of the year to ensure that client payments were received and supplier invoices were paid. We were successful in both cases. IRS was notified that the business was closed as of the end of the tax year 2017.

One big item was accomplished. Wrong! In June, 2018, I received a notice from the California Department of Tax and Fee Administration that my wife was on notice that she had not paid her sales tax or reported it to the Tax Board. Forty-five minutes and two telephone calls later I was able to talk with a representative who was most helpful and promised to close the account once she received a certified death certificate. When I asked, she returned the original to me.

> **If your loved one had a business, I hope with the help of professionals, the business will survive the death of the owner.**

In my case, my wife's business was small. If your loved one had a large successful business, I hope with the help of professionals, the business will survive the death of the owner. Again, planning and communications with all concerned is paramount.

In my case, surprises kept coming in the mailbox. Digital records were hidden in emails, texts and on-line accounts. Be careful to monitor your loved one's email accounts and text messages. Keep them active for a least one year.

FINAL THOUGHTS AND ACKNOWLEDGEMENTS

When I started writing this guide, I felt it would be a few pages long. I would send it to our friends so that, when the time came, the necessary information to travel the journey would be available. I hoped it would make their journey easier and less stressful than mine. Little did I know the guide would take on a life of its own. I am pleased you have a copy.

There are many people to thank for their help, ideas, and guidance. First thanks go out to my children, Leigh Speicher, Dr. Ted Speicher, and Jill Schlicher for their amazing support.

In no special order, professional help has been wonderful from Hospice of the East Bay in Northern California, Lafayette Orinda Presbyterian Church and their Grief Support Workshops and the Lamorinda Sunrise Rotary Club. Specific professional help was given by Certified Financial Advisors, Peggy Cabaniss (retired), Randal Kiessel, and Hays Englehart. Legal advice came from Charles A. "Cal" Lee and others. Insurance company information was provided by Don Jenkins. Other help came from Sam and Sandy D'Amico, tax advisor Daniel Levy, and Vicki Von Arx, a friend who lost her husband three years ago.

Additional help and guide ideas came from Dan Foley and some family members of my cousin who passed away soon after my wife. Connie Zook and Amy Satterfield were of valuable assistance especially when it came to the experiences with the credit card companies and their agreements.

There are a number of close friends that I leaned on during my journey. They all lost their wives at some point in the past. Special thanks go to Pat Flaharty and Gary Fulcher.

I also need to thank Gerald Chinen, Pastor, Congregational Care, at Lafayette Orinda Presbyterian Church in Lafayette, California who graciously allowed me to use portions of his guide for preparing for a memorial service and other documents that I felt would be of help to my readers.

As I mentioned in the Guide, my initial idea was a result of joining a grief support group at my church. I want to thank Beverly Fellows for her excellent job of facilitating the grief support group journey.

And finally, I need to thank my editor and proof reader, Julie Sullivan and layout expert, Molly Williams, Managing Editor of Big Hat Press, Lafayette, California. Julie was very understanding with me. I thought I was a fairly good writer, I was wrong. Julie had to use many pens with red ink to get my manuscript into readable form. Molly was able to get the formatting done for publication without too many comments about my writing skills. Thanks ladies for your wonderful help.

I am available by email to answer questions:

beforeandafterguide@gmail.com

I am not a professional, but if I do not have an answer for you, I'll try to find someone who does.

I am a living example of the statement, "Life will get better."

30698190R00035

Made in the USA
Lexington, KY
12 February 2019